DADDY GOES TO TREATMENT

BY BRITTANY PATRICK
ILLUSTRATED BY ALEX UHL

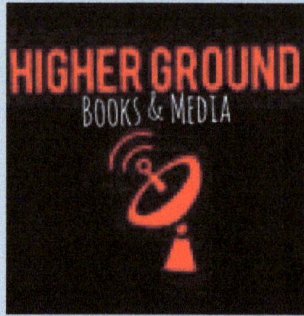

Higher Ground Books & Media
Springfield, Ohio.
http://highergroundbooksandmedia.com

Printed in the United States of America 2021

Dedication

This book is dedicated to Saige, Nyah, Zachary and my mom for loving me at my most difficult times, and never giving up on me, I'd be lost with out them.

Daddy had to make a phone call and answer a million questions,
but Mommy came to talk to me.

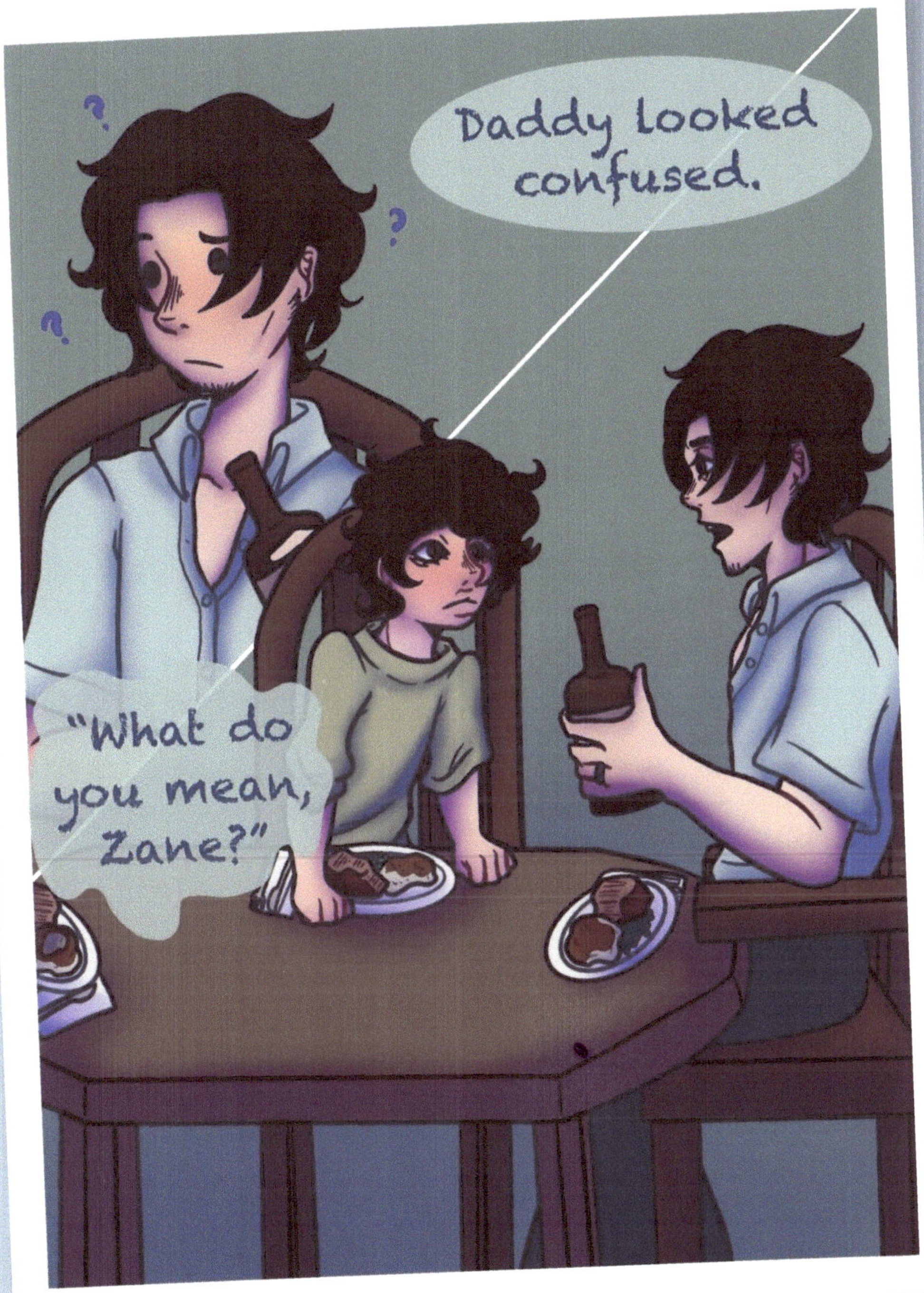
Daddy looked confused.
"What do you mean, Zane?"

"I understand, I don't like to be sick either,
so I take the yucky medicine the doctor gives me until I'm better."
"Wow, Zane, you're so smart, I'm glad you get it."

After dinner, we helped Daddy pack all his clothes, socks, underwear, pants, shirts, and everything.
"It's like you're going to a sleepover, Daddy!"
I said excitedly.
"Kind of, but its for 30 days."

"30 days, Daddy, that's a long time,
I can't even count to 30,"
I said.
Mommy laughed,
"I promise it will fly by, and Grandma is coming to watch you while I go to work."

After Daddy put the picture in the suitcase, we walked upstairs into my room.
I changed into my p.j.s then got in my bed, Daddy and Mommy read a book to me until I fell asleep.
PETER PAN

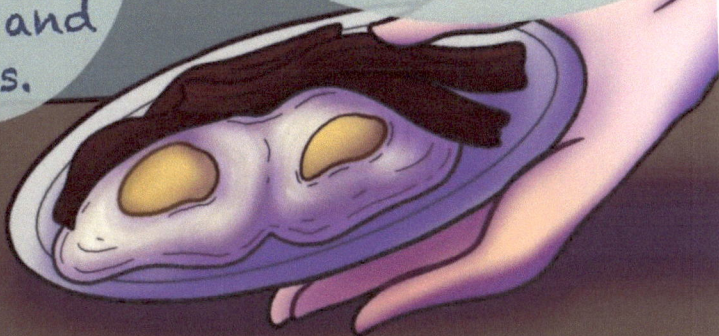

Mommy was crying, I could see the tears running down her cheek.
"What's wrong?"
I asked.

"Nothing is wrong, Zane,
I'm just so happy Daddy is going to get better, and we will have a normal life."
I hugged Mommy and gave her a big kiss.

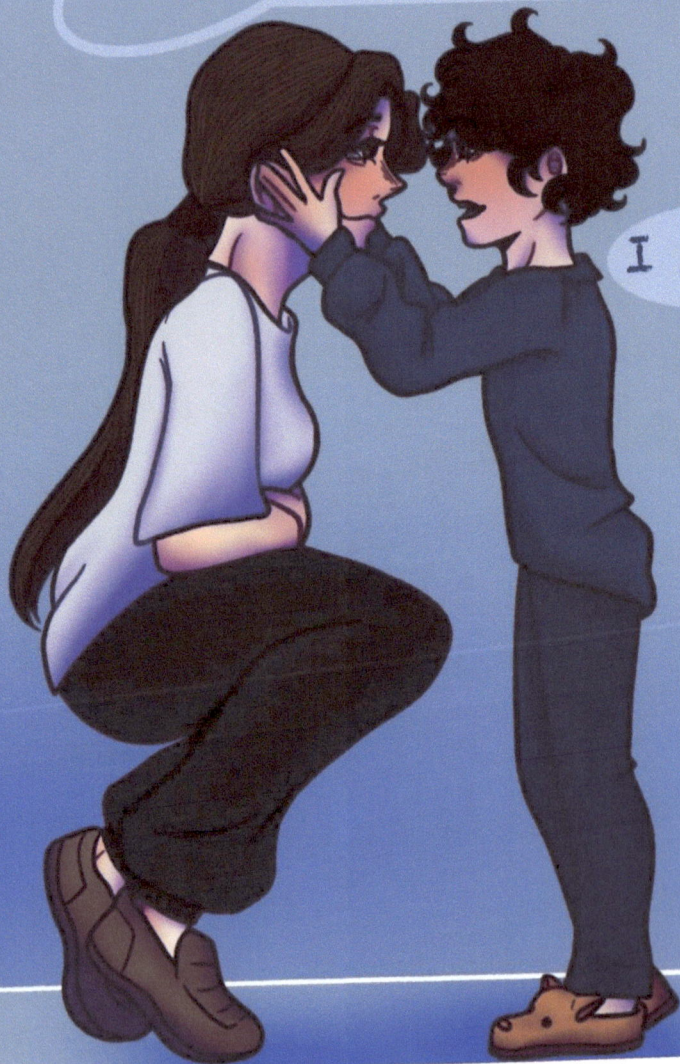

Other Titles Available from
Higher Ground Books & Media:

All the Scary Things by Rebecca Benston
That Bird Needs Glasses by Rebecca Benston
Grumble D. Grumble Learns to Smile by Rebecca
Benston
On a Hike with Pixie Trist and Bo by Charlotte Hopkins
Pixie Trist and Bo Explore the Ocean Floor by Charlotte Hopkins
The Tin Can Gang by Chuck David

Add these titles to your collection today!
www.highergroundbooksandmedia.com

Do you have a story to tell?

Higher Ground Books & Media is an independent Christian-based publisher specializing in stories of triumph! Our purpose is to empower, inspire, and educate through the sharing of personal experiences.

Please visit our website for our submission guidelines.

www.highergroundbooksandmedia.com

SPECIAL OFFERS FOR YOU!

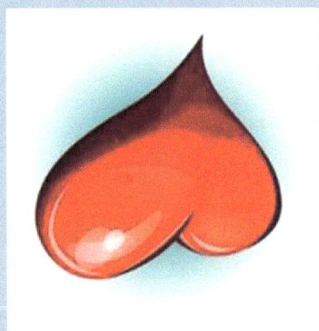

Save 20% on your first order in the
Higher Ground Books & Media Shop!

Just use the code: **NEWCUSTOMER** at checkout!

Thank you for your support!